WITH COMPLIMENTS

Chem-Science Laboratories (Pty) Ltd
P.O.Box 4618
Durban 4000
SOUTH AFRICA

Laboratories & Head Office at:

380 Umbilo Road
Glenwood
Durban 4001
kwaZulu-Natal
South Africa

Website: www.chemsciencelaboratories.com

A LABORATORY POCKET MANUAL

Vic Soffiantini, Chartered Chemist, M.R.S.C.

Editor

Italic Publisher Durban, South Africa

Published by:

Italic Publishers
P.O. Box 4618
Durban 4000
South Africa

Cover design by: SBG

First Edition 2009
Second Edition 2015
Reprint 2016
Third Edition 2018

Printed and Bound by: Lulu.com

Sales orders at: http://www.lulu.com

ISBN 978-1-291-42283-2

Editor's Note:

Disclaimer:

Every reasonable effort has been made to make this manual free of errors, but no warranty or fitness for use has been implied. The Editor and publisher shall have neither liability nor responsibility to any person, company or entity whatsoever, with respect to any loss or damages arising from the information contained in this manual.

For any errors noted or suggestions, please send an email message to info@laboratories.co.za

CONTENTS

Table 1

International System (SI) of Units

Property	Basic SI unit	Derived units
length	meter (m)	kilometre (km) centimetre (cm)
mass	kilogram (kg)	gram (g)
volume	cubic meter (m^3)	litre (L) millilitre (mL) cubic centimetre (cm^3, cc)
thermodynamic temperature	Kelvin (K)	Celsius (C)
energy	joule (J)	calorie (c) kilocalorie (kcal, C)
time	second (s)	millisecond (ms)
electric current	ampere (A)	milliamps (mA)
amount of substance	Mole (mol)	A Base unit of SI
luminous intensity	candela (cd)	A Base unit of SI

Table 2

International System of Derived Units

Property	Derived unit
frequency	hertz (Hz)
force	newton (N)
pressure	Pascal (Pa)
power	watt (W)
electric charge	coulomb (C)
emf, potential difference	volt (V)
capacitance	farad (F)
electric resistance	ohm (Ω)
electric conductance	Siemens (S)
electric inductance	henry (H)
magnetic flux	weber (Wb)
magnetic flux density	tesla (T)
luminous flux	lumen (lm)
luminance	lux (lx)
activity (radionuclide)	Becquerel (Bq)
adsorbed dose	gray (Gy)
dose equivalent	Sievert (Sv)
catalytic activity	katal (kat)
plane angle	radian (rad)
solid angle	steradian (sr)

Table 3

SI Prefixes

10^{24}	yotta	Y
10^{21}	zetta	Z
10^{18}	exa	E
10^{15}	peta	P
10^{12}	tera	T
10^{9}	giga	G
10^{6}	mega	M
10^{3}	kilo	k
10^{2}	hecto	h
10^{1}	deka	da
10^{-1}	deci	d
10^{-2}	centi	c
10^{-3}	milli	m
10^{-6}	micro	μ
10^{-9}	nano	n
10^{-12}	pico	p
10^{-15}	femto	f
10^{-18}	atto	a
10^{-21}	zepto	z
10^{-24}	yocto	y

$10^{0} = 1$	$10^{-0} = 1/10^{0} = 1/1 = 1$
$10^{1} = 10$	$10^{-1} = 1/10^{1} = 1/10 = 0.1$
$10^{2} = 100$	$10^{-2} = 0.01$

Table 4

Concentration Units

1 litre = 1 cubic decimetre (1dm^3) 1 ml = 1 cubic centimetre (1 cm^3) = 1 cc
1 parts per million = 1 ppm = 1 part solute in 1 000 000 parts solution
1 microgram/litre (μg/l) = 1 part per billion = 1 ppb (by volume) = 0.001 ppm (by volume)
1 ppm (by volume) = 1 mg/litre = 1 microgram/ml = 1 ng/microliter = 1 % m/v x 0.0001
1 ppm (by volume) = 1 cm^3/m^3 = 1 μl/litre
1 ppm (by weight) = 1 mg/kilogram = 1 microgram/g = 1 ng/mg = 1 % m/m x 0.0001
1% = 1 part solute per 100 parts solution
1% m/v = 1 mass part solute per 100 volume parts solution
1% m/m = 1 mass part solute per 100 mass parts solution
10% = 10 parts solute per 100 parts solution
1 gram/tonne (g/T) = 1 part per million (ppm) = 1 milligram/litre (mg/l)

1 + 1 = 1 part reagent A plus 1 part reagent B
1 : 1 = 1 part reagent A to 1 part solution B
1:10 = 1 part reagent A to 10 part solution = 10%

Table 5

Weight or Mass Units
(approximate)

1 kilogram (kg) = 1000 grams (g) = 15432grains
1 gram (g or gm) = 1000 milligrams (mg)
1 milligram (mg) = 1000 micrograms (µg)
1 microgram(µg or mcg)=1000nanograms(ng)
1 nanogram (ng) = 1000 picograms (pg)
1 gram x 0.03527 = 1 ounce Avoirdupois
1 gram = 15 grains Apothecary
1 dram = 4 gram = 60 grains Apothecary
1 grain = 0.0648 gram (g)
1 ounce (Apothecary) = 30 gram
1 ounce (Avoirdupois oz) = 16 drams (dr)
1 troy ounce (oz t) = 1 Apothecary ounce = 480 grains = 20 pennyweights (dwt)
1 metric carat = 200mg
1 pennyweight = 24 grains Avoirdupois = 1.555 grammes
1 kilogram (kg) = 2.2 pounds (lbs)
1 ounce x 28.35 = 1 gram
1 pound (lb) = 16 ounces = 453.59 grams (g or gm) = 7000 grains

Table 5 (continued)

Weight or mass units (approximate)

1 stone = 14 pounds (lb)
1 quarter = 28 pounds (lb)
1 kilogram = 32oz = 2 lb
1 kilogram (kg) x 2.2046 = 1 pound (lb)
1 kilogram (kg) x 35.27 = 1 long ounce
1 kilogram (kg) x 0.0009842 = 1 long ton
1 kilogram (kg) x 0.001102 = 1 short ton
1 long ton = 1 gross ton = 2240 pounds
1 cental (ctl) = 100 pounds
1 short ton = 1 net ton = 1 US ton = 2000 pounds
1 tonne = 1 metric ton = 2204.6 pounds
1 US ton (short ton) = 0.907185 tonne (t) = 0.892857 UK ton
1 hundred weight (cwt) = 112 pounds (lb) = 1792 ounzes (oz)
1 bushel US (bu) = 352.4 hectolitres (hl)
1 stone (st) = 907 kg = 0.9 ton US
1 part per billion (ppb) = 1 μg/kg
1 part per million (ppm) = 1 mg/kg

gram = gramme = g = gm = grm-----*but g also is for gravity, where g = 9.8 m/s^2 = 32.2 ft/s^2*

Table 6

Avoirdupois Weights

1 ounce (oz) = 16 drams (dr) = 28.3495 gram
1 pound (lb) = 16 oz = 7000 grains = 454 gram
1 dram (avoir.) = 1.7718 gram
1 stone = 14 lb = 6.35 kilogram
1 quarter = 28 lb = 12.701 kilogram (kg)
1 hundredweight (cwt) long = 112 lb = 50.80 kg
1 hundredweight (cwt)short = 110 lb = 45.36 kg
1 long ton = 2240 pounds (lbs) = 1.016 metric ton
1 short ton = 2000 lbs = 0.90718 metric tons
1 cental (ctl) = 100 pound (lb)
1 Troy ounce (oz t) = 1 Apothecaries' ounce
1 Apothecaries' ounce = 480 grains = 30 gram
1 Apothecaries' ounce = 20 pennyweights (dwt)
1 pennyweight (dwt) Troy = 24 grains = 1.55517 gram (g)
1 grain = 0.0648 gram (g)
1 dram (apoth.) = 60 grains = 4 g
1 scruple (apoth.) = 1.296 gram
1 drachm (apoth.) = 3.888 gram

Table 7

Length Units

1 inch (in) = 2.5400 centimetre (cm) = 25.4 mm
1 foot (ft) = 12 inches (in) =0.304 metres (m)
1 yard = 3 feet (ft) = 0.914 metres (m)
1 millimetre (mm) x 0.03937 = 1 inch
1 square centimetre x 0.155 = 1 square inch
1 metre (m) x 3.281 = 1 foot (ft) = 1.0936 yards
1 rod = 16½ ft = 5½ yds
1 furlong = 660 feet
1 metre = 39.37 inches
1 centimetre = 0.3937 inches
1 micron (μ) = 0.000001 metre = 0.001 millimetre
1 millimicron = ($m\mu$) = 0.001 micron
1 square metre x 10.7639 = 1 square foot
1 kilometre (km) x 0.6214 = 1 mile (Statute mile)
1 mile (mi) = 1760 yards (yd) = 320 rods
1 hand = 4 inches (in)
1 span = 9 inches (in)
1 link = 7.92 inches

Table 7 (continued)

Length Units

1 rod = 5.5 yards (yd)
1 pole = 5½ yards
1 fathom = 6 feet (ft)
1 chain = 22 yard = 4 rods = 100 links
1 furlong = 220 yards = 40 poles
1 mile = 1760 yards = 8 furlongs = 80 chains
1 UK nautical mile = 6080 feet = 1853 metre
1 International nautical mile = 1852 metre
1 league = 3 miles
1 yard (yd) = 3 feet (ft)
1 chain (ch) = 1 yard (yd) x 0.0455
1 chain (ch) = 1 cricket pitch
1 nanometre (nm) = 1 billionth of a metre
1 light year (ly) = 9.4605284×10^{15} meters

Table 7 (continued)

Length Units

1 Angstrom (Å) = 10^{-8} cm = 3.9370 x 10^{-9} inch
1 DNA molecule = +- 2 nanometres (nm)
Human hair = +- 75 000 nm (diameter)
Bacterium = +- 5 000 nm
Virus = +- 50 nm

Table 8

Volume Units
(approximate)

1 pint (pt) = 20 fluid ounces (fl oz) = 4 gills
1 cubic inch = 16.387 cubic centimetres (cc)
1 cubic yard (c yd) = 27 c ft = 0.76455 cubic metres
1 stere = 1 cubic metre = 35.315 cubic feet
1 cubic foot water weighs 62.335 lbs
1 quart (qt) = 2 pints (pt) = 32 fl.oz. US
1 gallon (gal) = 4 quarts = 128 fl.oz. US
1 gallon (US gal) = 3.7853 litre (*l*)
1 peck = 2 gallons = 8 quarts = 1 decalitre
1 cord = 128 cu ft
1 bushel (bu) = 8 gallons = 4 pecks
1 US pint = 16 fluid ounces = 0.28 litres
1 US gallon = 0.83268 Imperial gallon or UK gal
1 barrel (bbl) petroleum oil = 42 US gallons (1bbl=31½gal)
1 hogshead (hhd) = 2 barrels
1 fl oz Apothecary = 30 ml
1 fl dram Apothecary = 4 ml
1 ml = 15 minims
1 gill (gl) = ¼ pint = 5 fluid oz = 150 ml
1 litre = 1000ml = 1.75 pints
1 tablespoon (Tbsp)= 20ml (15ml US)
1 teaspoon (tsp) = 5ml
1 cup = 250ml

Table 9

Area Units

(approximate)

1 square foot (ft^2) = 144 square inches (in^2) = 929 square centimetres
1 square yard (yd^2) = 9 ft^2 (sq ft)
1 acre = 4840 yd^2 = 4047 square metres = 4 roods = 10 square chains = 40.47 ares
1 rood = ¼ acre = 40 sq rods = 0.10 hectare
1 are = 1 dkm^2 = 0.0247 acre = 100 sq metres
1 square mile = 640 acres = 2.59 square (sq) kilometres = 25900 ares
1 acre = 160 sq rods
1 morgen = 2.11695 acres
1 Cape square foot = 1.0670 square foot
1 square inch (sq in) = 6.4516 square centimetres
1 sq cm = 0.1550 sq in
1 are (dkm^2) =119.6 sq yds
1 hectare (hm^2) =2.471 acres = 100 ares

Table 10

Temperature Scales

°C = °Celsius = °Centigrade = (°F-32) x 5/9
°F = °Fahrenheit = (9/5 x °C) + 32
Absolute zero = -273.15°C
Absolute scale = Kelvin scale = °C + 273.15
°Reaumur = 5/4 x °C
°Reaumur = (°F-32) x 4/9
°Rankine = °R = (°C + 273.15) x 9/5

The International Temperature Scale of 1990 is based on 16 fixed thermodynamic points, from -259.34°C to 1084.62°C

Table 11

Rate of Flow Units
(approximate)

1 litre/minute (lpm) x 0.03532 = 1 cubic foot/minute (cu ft/min)
1 litre/minute (lpm) = 0.22 gallon/minute
1 litre/minute (lpm) x 0.2642 = 1 gallon(US)/minute
1 m^3/s = 3.6 x 10^6 litres/hour
1 m^3/day = 0.6944 litre/min (lpm)
1 m^3/h = 0.2778 l/s
1 gal/min = 0.2727 m^3/h (cubic metres per hour)
I lpm = 60 l/h (litres per hour)

Table 12

Pressure Units

1 psi = 1 lbf/in^2 = 144 lbf/ft^2
1 psi = 2.310 ft head water at 20'C
1 psi = 0.704 meters water
1 psi = 27.7 inches water
1 psi = 0.0700 kg/cm^2
1 psi = 2.043 inches Hg at 20'C= 51.88mmHg
1 psi = 5.188 cm Hg = 51.71 mm Hg
1 psi = 0.0690 bar = 6.895 kN/m^2
1 psi = 68.947 millibar (mbar) = 6.895 kPa
1 bar = 10^5 N/m^2
1 N/m^2 = 1 Pascal = 10 dyn/cm^2
1 kiloPascal (kPa) = 0.14504 psi
1 kPa = 7.5006 mm of Hg
1 mm Hg = 0.019337 psi = 0.13595 cm of H$_2$0
1 bar = 14.50 lbf/in^2 = 14.50 psi
1 bar = 1.02 kgf/cm^2 = 0.9869 atm.
1 kgf/cm^2 = 1 kP/cm^2 = 1 technical atm
1 atm = 762.5 mm Hg
1 lbf/ft^2 = 0.4788 mbar = 0.3591 mm Hg

Table 13

Autoclave Steam Pressure & Temperature

Steam pressure (lbs/sq.in.)	Temperature (°C)	Temperature (°F)
0	100	212
2	104	219
5	108	227
8	113	235
10	115	239
12	118	244
15	**121**	**250**
18	124	255
20	126	259
22	128	262
25	130	267
28	133	271
30	135	274

Table 14

Vacuum Units
(approximate)

1 mbar = 1 x 10^{-3} = 0.75 torr = 1 x 10^{-3} atm
1 bar = 1 x 105 Pa = 1 atm = 14.5 lbf.in^{-2}
1 torr = 1.333mbar = 1mm Hg = 13.6mm H_2O
1 Pa = 1 Nm^{-2} = 0.01 mbar = 7.5 x 10^{-3} torr
1atm =30in Hg = 14.7 lbf.in^{-2} = 1x10^4mm H_2O
1 lbf.in^{-2} = 2 in Hg = 52 torr = 69 mbar
1 kgf.cm^{-2} = 1 x 10^4 mm H_2O = 14.2 lbf.in^{-2}
1 in Hg = 25.4 mm Hg = 25.4 torr = 34 mbar
1 mm Hg =13.6 mm H_2O = 133 Pa = 1 torr
1 in H_2O = 2.5 mbar = 2.5 x 10^{-3} kgf.cm^{-2}
1 mm H_2O = 9.8 x 10^{-5}bar = 3 x 10^{-3} in Hg
1 mm Hg = 0.0394 in. Hg = 1.33 kPa
1 mm Hg = 0.01934 psi
10^{-3} to 10^{-7} mbar = high vacuum
1 mbar to 1 bar = medium vacuum

Table 15

Acid Factors

1.0ml of N/10 (0.1M) NaOH standardised titrimetric (i.e. a decinormal) solution equivalent to:

0.004603g **formic acid** HCOOH (a monocarboxylic acid)
0.009008g **lactic acid** $C_3H_6O_3$(an organic acid)
0.003646g **hydrochloric acid** HCl (monoprotic mineral acid)
0.004904g **sulphuric acid** H_2SO_4(a diprotic mineral acid)
0.006005g **acetic acid** CH_3COOH (a monocarboxylic acid)
0.007005g **citric acid monohydrate** $C_3H_4(OH)(COOH)_3.H_2O$ (a tricarboxylic acid)
0.00640g **citric acid anhydrous** $C_3H_4(OH)(COOH)_3$ (a tricarboxylic acid)
0.005804g **maleic acid** $C_2H_2(COOH)_2$(a dicarboxylic acid)
0.006706g **malic acid** $C_2H_3OH(COOH)_2$(a dicarboxylic acid)
0.028245g **oleic acid** (for tallows and fish oil $C_{18}H_{34}O_2$) (a monounsaturated fatty acid)
0.007504g **tartaric acid** $C_2H_2(OH)_2(COOH)_2$(a dicarboxylic acid)
0.0256g **palmitic acid** (for palm oil) $C_{16}H_{32}O_2$(a saturated fatty acid)
0.0200g **lauric acid** (for crude and refined palm kernel and coconut oils) $C_{12}H_{24}O_2$(a saturated fatty acid)
0.012210g **benzoic acid** $C_7H_6O_2$(an organic acid)
0.006303g **oxalic acid** dihydrate $(COOH)_2.2H_2O$ (a dicarboxylic acid)
0.003266g o-**phosphoric acid** H_3PO_4 (a triprotic acid)
0.017613g L- **ascorbic acid** $C_6H_8O_6$(an organic acid)

Table 16

Vitamin Names

Vitamin	Chemical
A (A1,A2)	Retinol, Retinal, Retinoic acid
A precursor	beta-Carotene
B1	Thiamine
B2	Riboflavin
B3	Niacin, Nicotinic acid
B4	Choline
B5	Pantothenic acid
H (part of B complex)	Biotin
B6	Pyridoxine, Pyrldoxal, Pyrldoxamine
B9	Folic acid, Folate, Folacin
B12	Cobalamin, Cyanocobalamine
C	Ascorbic acid
D	Calciferol,
E	alpha-Tocopherol
K (K1,K2,K3)	Phylloquinone, Menadione
P	bioflavonoids

Table 17

Amino Acids Names

Amino Acid, with letter codes
alanine - ala - A
arginine - arg - R
asparagine - asn - N
aspartic acid - asp - D
cysteine - cys - C)
glutamine - gln - Q
glutamic acid - glu - E
glycine - gly - G
histidine - his - H
isoleucine - ile - I
leucine - leu - L
lysine - lys - K
methionine - met - M
phenylalanine - phe - F
proline - pro - P
serine - ser - S
threonine - thr - T
tryptophan - trp - W
tyrosine - tyr - Y
valine - val - V

Table 18

Fatty Acids Names

Structure	Name
C3:0	Propionic acid
C4:0	Butyric acid
C5:0	Valeric acid
C6:0	Caproic acid
C8:0	Caprylic acid
C10:0	Capric acid
C12:0	Lauric acid
C14:0	Myristic acid
C14:1	Myristoleic acid
C16:0	Palmitic acid
C16:1	Palmitoleic acid / sapienic acid
C17:0	Margaric acid
C17:1	Heptadecenoic acid
C18:0	Stearic acid
C18:1	Oleic acid / elaidic acid / vaccenic acid (omega-9)
C18:2	Linoleic acid / linoelaidic acid (omega-6)
C18:3	Linolenic acid (omega-3)
C20:0	Arachidic acid
C20:1	Gadoleic acid
C20:2	Eicosadienoic acid
C20:4	Arachidonic acid (omega-6)
C20:5	Eicospentaenoic acid (omega-3)
C22:0	Behenic acid
C22:1	Erucic acid
C22:2	Brassic acid
C22:6	Docosahexaenoic acid (omega-3)
C24:0	Lignoceric acid
C24:1	Nervonic acid

Table 19

Vegetable oils

Oil	Smoke Point °C	Auto-ignition °C	Major fatty acid
Almond	220		oleic,linoleic
Canola (rapeseed)	230	380	oleic,linoleic
Coconut	180	330	lauric,myristic
Corn (maize)	220		linoleic,oleic
Cottonseed	210	350	linoleic,palmitic
Flaxseed (linseed oil)	110		linolenic,oleic
Grape seed	200		linoleic,oleic
Groundnut (peanut)	230	350	oleic,linoleic
Macadamia	200	370	oleic,palmitoleic
Olive	180	430	oleic
Palm	230	340	palmitic,oleic
Pecan	240		oleic,linoleic
Safflower	250		linoleic
Sesame	220		linoleic,oleic
Soybean	240	390	linoleic,oleic
Sunflower	230	340	linoleic
Tung		460	linolenic
Walnut	180		linoleic,oleic

Table 20

Calorie Factors
(approximate)

Carbohydrates, as monosaccharides = 3.8kcal per 100gram = 16.5kJ per 100gram
Glycitol = 3.8kcal per 100gram = 16kJ per 100gram
Proteins = 4.0kcal per 100gram = 17kJ per 100gram
Alcohol, as ethanol = 7.0kcal per 100gram = 29kJ per 100gram
Fats and oils = 9.0kcal per 100gram = 37kJ per 100gram
Sugar alcohols = 2.4kcal per 100gram = 10kJ per 100gram
Organic acids = 3.0kcal per 100gram = 13kJ per 100gram
Citric acid = 4.1kcal per 100gram = 17kJ per 100gram

Where: *kcal is kilocalorie*
            kJ is kiloJoule

Table 20 (continued)

Calorie Factors

1 calorie (cal) = 4.184 joules (J).
1 kilocalorie (kcal) = 4.184 kilojoules (kJ).
1 food Calories (Cal) = 4.184 kilojoules = kilocalories (note the capital C).
1000 kilojoules (kJ) = 1 megajoules (MJ).
Total Food Energy in Calories/100gram = (3.8 x %carbohydrates) + (4.0 x %protein)+(9.0 x %fat)
Total Food Energy value in kJ/100gram or in kJ/100ml= (16.5 x %carbohydrates) + (17 x %protein) + (37x %fat)

Where: *kcal is kilocalorie*
              kJ is kiloJoule

The unit of energy in the SI system is the joule.

Table 21

IR Absorbance peaks

Functional group	Wavenumber Band, in cm^{-1}
C-H	+_ 3000
C=O	1630 to 1850
O-H	3400 to 3650
Carboxylic acids O-H	2500 to 3000
Aromatics	1600 to 2000
C≡N	2100 to 2260
C≡C	2100 to 2260
C-O	1050 to 1150
C=C	1620 to 1680
Alcohols, phenols: O-H	3200 to 3550
Amines N-H	3500 to 3700
Nitriles C≡N	2220 to 2260
Aldehydes & ketones C=O	1740 to 1690
Carboxylic acids C=O	1710 to 1780
Amides N-H	3500 to 3700
Amides C=O	1630 to 1690

Table 22

Formulae

Formulae for cleaning glassware

1. *Formula for chromic Acid* (HAZARDOUS CHEMICAL):
Ideal for inorganic dirt, mineral residues, calcium hardness deposits, etc.
25g sodium dichromate dissolved in 25ml water and add SLOWLY concentrated sulphuric acid with stirring to final volume of about 1 litre...............evolution of heat!
2. *Formula for Alcoholic Caustic* (HAZARDOUS CHEMICAL): *ideal for organic dirt, fats, oils, foodstuffs, etc.*
Approximately 56g potassium hydroxide dissolved in minimum water, then add alcohol (methylated spirits) to make up to about 1 litre (i.e. +-1N alcoholic KOH).
CAUTION: do not soak glass items for longer than 30 minutes in this solution.
3. *Formula for EXTRA effective general detergent:*
Add about 10ml hydrofluoric acid (HAZARDOUS CHEMICAL) to about 1litre general household dishwasher liquid. Mix well.
CAUTION: do not soak glass items for longer than 30 minutes in this solution.

Table 22 (continued)

Formula for cleaning sintered glass crucibles

Boil gently in aqua regia (3 parts hydrochloric acid + one part nitric acid) (HAZARDOUS CHEMICAL). Then flush crucible well with water whilst under vacuum filtration.

Formulae for sanitizing bench surfaces, etc.

70% alcohol; or

75% alcohol + 2% ether + 1% acetone + balance water. Do not apply to plastics.

Table 23

Sintered-glass filter crucible sizes

Porosity Grade Number	Porosity in microns (Pore Size Index)	ISO designation
0 (very coarse, fast filtering)	160-250	P250
1 (coarse)	100-160	P160
2 (medium)	40-100	P100
3 (medium)	16-40	P40
4 (fine, slow filtering)	10-16	P16

Table 24

Filter Paper and Funnel Sizes

Diameter of paper, in cm	Maximum capacity of filter, in ml	Filter Funnel size, in mm (top diameter)
7	8	45
9	10	55
11	20	70
12.5	30	80
15	70	90 or 100
18.5	130	110
24	300	150
32	400	200

Table 25

Whatman Filter Paper Properties

Whatman Number	Filtration rate	Particle retention size, (μm) (microns)	Some general uses
1	fast flow	11	general, air pollution
2	medium	8	general, coarse
3	medium	6	for Buchner funnels
4	fast flow	20-25	general, air pollution
5 or 6	slow	3	fine particle filtration
40	med. flow	8	gravimetric analyses, AAS
41	fast flow	20-25	large particles & gelatinous
42	slow flow	2.5	small particles such as barium sulphate
43	medium	16	soils and foodstuffs
44	slow	3	fine particle filtration
50	slow	2.7	not suitable for acid/alkalis
52	medium	7	for Buchner funnels
54	fast flow	20-25	not suitable for acid/alkalis
91	fast flow	>25	e.g. sugar tests or schoolwork

Table 25 (continued)

Whatman Filter Paper Properties

Whatman Number	Filtration rate	Particle retention	Some general uses
113 (crepe paper)	fast flow	30	wet-strengthened, general work
540 (acid resistant hardened paper)	medium flow	8	same as #40, metals, acid solutions, most common use.
541 (acid resistant hardened paper)	fast flow	20-25	acid/alkali solutions, proteins & fibre foodstuffs
542 (acid resistant hardened paper)	slow flow	2.7	same as #42, acid solutions
1 PS (silicone coated)	-	water repellent	aqueous/organic phase separations
GF/A (glass fibre)	-	1.6	air pollution
GF/B (glass fibre)	-	1.0	very fine particles
GF/C (glass fibre)	-	1.2	water analyses
GF/D (glass fibre)	-	2.7	coarse particles
GF/F (glass fibre)	-	0.7	very fine particles

It is recommended to always use hardened ashless filter papers when doing quantitative analytical work, e.g. Whatman #541 or its equivalent, instead of Whatman #41.

Table 26

Filter Paper Equivalents

Whatman Number	MN (Macherey Nagel)	Albet	MFS /Advantec	S & S (Schleicher & Schuell)
1 or 93	645 or 615	400 or 412	2 or 231	591-A or 597
2	616md	413	232	593
3	618	415	131	818 or 593-A
4	617	411	1	604
5	-	414	235	602 h
6		416	131	593-A
40	640m	145	5B	589 white
41	640 we	135	5A	589 black
42	640 de	150	5C	589 red
43	640m	140	7	589 green
44		140	6	589 blue
50		501	4A	576 or 577
52	1672	502	-	1574
54	1670	503	-	1573
114	1670	503	-	
540	1640 md	1145	-	1506
541	1640 we	1135	-	1505
542	1640 de	1150	-	1507

Table 27

Viscometers

Viscometer	Some uses	Units
Capillary, glass,kinematic:	oils	Centipoises or mm2/s
U-Tube		
U-Tube Reverse	black oils	
Suspended Level		
Ubbelohde		
Cannon-Fenske		
Ostwald		
Ford Cups	Petroleum oils	seconds
Redwood	**obsolete**	seconds
Falling Ball type:		seconds
Hoeppler	molasses	
Haake	polymers	
Benson		
Brookfield	Paints, polymers, inks,	

Viscosity changes with temperature, hence temperature recording is critical

Table 28

Hydrometers

Hydrometer	Some uses	Units
Alcoholmeter	alcohol content in beverages	% alcohol by volume
Syke's (or Cartier's)	Alcohol content	% alcohol by volume
Salinometer	salt (NaCl) content in brine solutions	°S
Balling (Plato)	sugar in brewing	Degrees wort extract
Lactometer, Quevenne	dissolved solids in milk or skim milk	%
Soxhlet's Lactometer	Density of milk	25° to 35° (SG)
Brix	% sugar by mass in juices	°B
Twaddle	densities greater than water, e.g. strength of H_2SO_4	°TW
Density	density of solutions	g/ml or kg/l
Specific Gravity (SG)	Relative density solutions greater than water	(no units as SG is a ratio of two densities)
API Gravity	SG of petroleum products	°API
Baume'	SG of solutions	°Be'
Oleometer	Weight & density of vegetable oils	degrees
Ammoniameter	Density ammonia solutions	0° to 40°

Note: °B also is Balling Saccharometer units.

The type of hydrometer to be used is dependent upon the physical properties (surface tension) of the liquid being measured.

Table 29

Hydrometer Conversions

Baumé degrees = °Be = 145 – 145/SG   *for liquids heavier than water*
°Be = (140/SG) - 130 *for liquids lighter than water*
Specific Gravity or SG = Relative Density
°API = (141.5/SG) – 131.5
Twaddel degrees = °TW = 200 (SG – 1)   *for liquids heavier than water*
SG of liquid at T°C/4°C = $\dfrac{\text{density of liquid at T°C}}{\text{density water at 4°C}}$ = $\dfrac{\text{density of liquid at T°C}}{0.999973}$ = 1.0000   = density of liquid at T°C

Some density conversions:

1 lb/cu ft = 0.1337 lb/gal = 0.016g/cm^3 = 16.019 g/l
1 lb/gal = 7.481 lb/cu ft = 0.1198 g/cm^3 = 119.83 g/l
1 g/cm^3 = 0.03613 lb/cu in = 62.43 lb/cu ft = 10^3 g/l

Table 30

Density of Water
(True density, in vacuo)
(density by hydrometer)

Temperature °C	Density g/cm^3
-4	0.999450 (lower density)
0	0.999841
3.98	0.999973 (most dense)
4	0.999972
8	0.999849
10	0.999700
15	0.999099
16	0.998943
20	0.998203
22	0.997770
24	0.997296
25	0.99704
26	0.996783
28	0.996232
30	0.995646

Table 31

Density of 10% m/m aqueous solutions

Chemical Solution	Density, true, at 20 °C (g/cm³)
Ammonia (NH_4OH)	0.957
Ammonium chloride (NH4Cl)	1.028
Calcium chloride ($CaCl_2$)	1.084
Copper sulphate ($CuSO_4$)	1.107
Ethanol (alcohol)	0.982
Formaldehyde (HCHO)	1.028
Glycerine ($C_3H_8O_3$)	1.022
Hydrochloric acid (HCl)	1.050
Methanol (CH_3OH)	0.982
Nitric acid (HNO_3)	1.054
Phosphoric acid (H_3PO_4)	1.053
Sodium carbonate (Na_2CO_3)	1.103
Sodium chloride (NaCl)	1.071
Sodium hydroxide (NaOH)	1.109
Sodium sulphate ($NaSO_4.10H_2O$)	1.040
Sulphuric acid (H_2SO_4)	1.066
Zinc chloride ($ZnCl_2$)	1.089
Zinc sulphate ($ZnSO_4.7H_2O$)	1.058

Table 32

Volume Correction Factors, Density Factors and Stowage Factors

Commodity	VCF (per °C)	SF (m³/ton)
Coke Breeze	-	1.9 - 2.8
Gas oil	0.00067	
Fuel oil	0.00063	
Jet fuel	0.00072-74	
Mogas (petrol)	0.00067	
Fish oil	0.00058-73	
Poultry fat	0.00068	
Vegetable oils	0.00068	
Soyabean oil	0.00069	
Palm kernel oil	0.00071	
RBD Palm olein	0.00069	
Molasses, blackstrap (cane)	0.00057	
Water	0.00025	1.0
Coal	-	1.4
Grains	-	1.3
Glycerine	0.00061	
Acid oil	0.00068	
Tallow	0.00068	
Linseed oil	0.00068	

SF in ft³/ton = SF in m³/ton x 35.31

SF in m³/ton = 1/kg/l

Table 33

Redox (Reduction-Oxidation) Reagents

REAGENT SOLUTION	MOST COMMON CONCENTRATION IN MOL L^{-1}
Ammonium ceric sulphate	0.10
Ceric sulphate	0.10
Ferroin	0.025
Iodine	0.50
Potassium bromate-bromide	0.0167
Potassium dichromate	0.0167
Potassium iodate	0.05
Potassium permanganate	0.20
Sodium arsenite	0.05
Sodium thiosulphate	0.10

Table 34

Redox (Reduction-Oxidation) Indicators

INDICATOR	REDOX POTENTIAL VOLTS E_0 @ 20°C, pH 7	COLOUR CHANGE Oxidised form - Reduced form	PREPARATION
Barium diphenylamine-4-sulphonate	+0.83	Red - colourless	0.005 Molar Solution in water
Diphenylamine	+0.76	blue - colourless	Dissolve 1g in 100ml conc sulphuric acid
Ferroin (1,10 phenanthroline ferrous complex)	+1.1	blue - orange red	Dissolve 0.7g ferrous sulphate + 1.5g 1,10 0-phenanthroline in 100ml water
Indophenol (2,6 dichlorophenol)	+0.2	blue - colourless	Dissolve 0.2g of the sodium salt dehydrate in 100ml water
Methylene Blue	+0.53	blue - colourless	Dissolve 0.2g in 100ml water
Neutral Red	-0.3	violet/red - colourless	Dissolve 0.5g in 100ml alcohol
Safranin T	-0.29	blue violet or brown - colourless	Dissolve 0.5g in 100ml water
Starch	specific in iodine titrations	blue - colourless	Add 1g soluble starch paste to 100ml boiling water, stir well
Xylene Cyanol FF	+1.05	yellow - pink	Xylene Cyanol FF

Table 35

Neutralisation (Acid-Base) Indicators

INDICATOR	pH RANGE	COLOUR CHANGE acid -alkali	PREPARATION
Alizarin	5.5 – 6.8	yellow - red	0.1% in methanol
Bromocresol purple	5.2 - 6.8	yellow -purple	0.04g in 100ml of 20% alcohol
Bromophenol Blue	2.9 - 4.6	yellow – red violet	0.04g in 100ml of 20% alcohol
Bromocresol Green	3.7 - 5.3	yellow - blue	0.1g in 14.3ml 0.01M NaOH+236ml water
Cresol Red	0.4 - 1.8 7.0 – 8.8	red-yellow yellow - red	0.1g in 26.2ml 0.01M NaOH+224ml water
Congo Red	3.0 – 5.0	blue - scarlet	0.1% in water
Litmus	5.0 - 8.0	red - blue	paper strips
Methyl Orange	3.0 - 4.5	red – yellow orange	0.1g in 100ml water
Methyl Red	4.3 - 6.2	red – orange yellow	0.02g in 100ml alcohol
Neutral Red	6.8 - 8.0	red - orange	0.01g in 50 ml alcohol + 50 ml water
Phenol Red	6.6 - 8.3	yellow - red	0.05g in 100ml 20% alcohol
Phenolphthalein	8.2 - 9.8	colourless - red	1.0g in 100ml 60% alcohol
Thymol Blue	1.2 - 2.8 8.0 - 9.6	red - yellow yellow - blue	0.04g in 100ml of 20% alcohol
Thymolphthalein	9.4 – 10.4	colourless - blue	0.04 g in 50 ml alcohol + 50 ml water

Table 36

Adsorption (Precipitation) Indicators

INDICATOR	COLOUR CHANGE	PREPARATION
Alizarin Red S	yellow - pink	0.2g sodium alizarin sulfonate in 100ml water
Bromophenol Blue	colourless - blue	Dissolve 0.1g in 100ml water
Fluorescein	yellow-green - red	Dissolve 0.2g in 100ml 70% alcohol
2,7 dichlorofluorescein	yellowish-pink	Dissolve 1g in 1L 70%alcohol
Eosin	pink – reddish	Dissolve 0.2g in 100ml 70% alcohol
Potassium chromate	yellow-orange brown	4.2g pot.chromate + 0.7g pot.dichromate in 100ml water
Rose Bengal	pink - bluish	Buy commercial
Tartrazine	colourless – yellow	Buy commercial

Table 37

Complexometric (EDTA) Indicators

INDICATOR	COLOUR CHANGE	PREPARATION
Calmagite	blue - red	Dissolve 0.5g in 100ml water.
Calcein (Fluorescein)	-	Purchase commercial product
Eriochrome Black T	blue - red	Dissolve 0.2g in 15ml ethanolamine + 5ml alcohol.
Murexide	blue	Suspend 0.5g in water.
Patton & Reeder's Reagent (HHSNNA)	wine red- blue	Purchase commercial product
Thorin Solution	yellow - pink	0.2% w/v
Xylenol Orange	yellow- red	Dissolve 0.5g in 100ml water.

Table 38

Mixed (Screened) Indicators

INDICATOR	pH RANGE	Colour change	PREPARATION
Screened Methyl Orange	2.9-4.4	Magenta -grey-green	Equal vols of 0.2% methyl orange + 0.3% Xylene cyanol FF, in 50% alcohol
Screened Methyl Red	4.2-6.3	Magenta -grey-green	Equal vols of 0.2% alc methyl red + 0.1% aq methylene blue
Bromocresol Green/Methyl Red	4.2-5.2	Pink-grey-green	Equal vols of 0.15% alc bromocresol green + 0.1% alc methyl red

Table 39

Hazardous Redox Chemicals

NEVER STORE ANY OXIDISING CHEMICAL NEXT TO ANY REDUCING CHEMICAL

List of some oxidising chemicals (not in order)	List of some reducing chemicals (not in order)
chlorates	ammonia, ammonium hydroxide
chromates	carbon
dichromates	metals
halogens	metal hydrides
hydrogen peroxide	nitrites
nitric acid	organic compounds
nitrates	phosphorus
perchlorates, persulphates	silicon
peroxides	sulphur
permanganates	

Table 40

Oxidation States

Element	Group	Atomic Number	Oxidation State
Li	1 (IA)	3	**+1**
Be	2 (IIA)	4	**+2**
B	13 (III)	5	**+3**, -1, +1, +2
C	14(IV)	6	**+4, -4**, +2
N	15 (V)	7	**-3**, +2 , +3, +4, +5
O	16 VI)	8	**-2**, -1, +1, +2
F	17 (VII)	9	**-1**
Na	1 (IA)	11	**+1,** -1
Mg	2 (IIA)	12	**+2**, +1
Al	13 (III)	13	**+3**, +1
Si	14(IV)	14	**+4, -4**, -1, -2, -3, +1, +2, +3
P	15 (V)	15	**-3, +3, +5**, +4
S	16 VI)	16	**-2**, +2, +4, +6
Cl	17 (VII)	17	**-1**, +1, +3, +5, +7
K	1 (IA)	19	**+1**
Ca	2 (IIA)	20	**+2**
Cr	6 (VI)	24	**+3, +6**
Mn	7 (VII)	25	**+2, +4, +7**
Fe	8 (VIII)	26	**+2, +3**, +4, +6
Co	9 (VIII)	27	**+2, +3**
Ni	10 (VIII)	28	**+2**
Cu	11 (IB)	29	**+2**, +1, +3, +4
Zn	12 (IIB)	30	**+2**
Mo	6 (VI)	42	**+4**, +6
I	17 (VII)	53	**-1**, +1, +5. +7
Pb	14 (IV)	82	**+2**, +4
Bi	15 (V)	83	**+3**, +5

Table 41

Preparation of 1 LITRE Volumetric Standard Solutions

The following solutions are <u>made up to 1 litre</u> volume with pure water:

Standard Solution	chemical used for preparation of Standard	Standardise against: (primary standard)	Indicator solution to be used	Approx. titration (Example only)
0.1N NaOH 0.1M NaOH 0.1 mol.l⁻¹ NaOH	4.00g NaOH pellets	±0.3g potassium hydrogen phthalate (as is)	phenolphthalein	12ml
1N NaOH 1M NaOH 1 mol.l⁻¹ NaOH	41g NaOH pellets	±1.0g potassium hydrogen phthalate (as is)	phenolphthalein	5ml
0.1N HCl 0.1M HCl 0.1 mol.l⁻¹ HCl	9.33ml of HCl of SG 1.16; or 8.3ml of HCl of SG 1.19	±0.2g Sodium tetraborate decahydrate (as is)	methyl red	12ml
1N HCl 1M HCl 1 mol.l⁻¹ HCl	93.3ml of HCl of SG 1.16; or 83ml of HCl of SG 1.19	±1.0g Sodium tetraborate decahydrate (as is)	methyl red	5ml
0.1N H_2SO_4 0.05M H_2SO_4 0.05 mol.l⁻¹ H_2SO_4	5.0g H_2SO_4 of SG 1.84	±0.2g Sodium tetraborate decahydrate (as is)	methyl red	12ml

Table 42

Standardisation of Volumetric Standard Solutions

How to calculate the exact strength of the Standard Solutions using primary standards in the titrations

---

For NaOH solutions (using potassium hydrogen phthalate):

$$N \text{ (or M)} = \frac{\text{g } C_8H_5KO_4}{0.20423 \times \text{ml titration}}$$

For HCl solutions (using sodium tetraborate):

$$N \text{ (or M)} = \frac{\text{g } Na_2B4O_7.10H_2O}{0.19072 \times \text{ml titration}}$$

For H₂SO₄ solutions (using sodium tetraborate):

$$N \text{ (or M)} = \frac{\text{g } Na_2B4O_7.10H_2O}{0.19072 \times \text{ml titration}}$$

Table 43

Strengths of common Concentrated Acids

Acid	% by weight	Density or SG	Approx. strength in mol/l or M	Approx. strength in N	Vol
Acetic acid, glacial	100	1.06	18	18	60
Acetic acid	96	1.06	17	17	63
Formic acid	98 - 100	1.22	26	26	39
Hydrochloric acid	36	1.18	12	12	87
Hydrochloric acid	32 - 34	1.16	10	10	100
Hydrochloric acid fuming	37 - 38	1.19	12.5	12.5	86
Hydrofluoric acid	48	1.14	28	28	36
Hydrofluoric acid	40	1.13	23	23	44
Nitric acid, fuming	99 - 100	1.52	21	21	44

Table 43 (continued)

Strengths of common Concentrated Acids

Acid	% by weight	Density or SG	Approx. strength in mol/l or M	Approx. strength in N	Vol
Perchloric acid	70	1.67	12	12	85
Perchloric acid	60	1.53	9	9	109
Phosphoric acid, ortho	89	1.75	16	48	63
Phosphoric acid, ortho	85	1.71	15	45	68
Sulphuric acid, fuming (oleum)	110	1.99	-	-	-
Sulphuric acid	95 - 98	1.84	18	36	55

Where:

Vol = ml acid required to make 1litre approximate 1.0M strength (1.0 mol/l) acid.

Table 44

Equivalents of Standard Test Sieves

Internal mesh width mm	US ASTM E-11	Mesh Number Tyler mesh/inch	BS 410 mesh/inch
0.037	400	400	
0.044	325	325	
0.045			350
0.053	270	270	300
0.063	230	250	240
0.074	200	200	
0.075			200
0.088	170	170	
0.090			170
0.105	140	150	150
0.125	120	115	120
0.149	100	100	
0.150			100
0.177	80	80	
0.180			85
0.210	70	65	72
0.250	60	60	60
0.297	50	48	
0.300			52
0.354	45	42	

Table 44 (continued)

Equivalents of Standard Test Sieves

Internal mesh width mm	US ASTM E-11	Mesh Number Tyler mesh/inch	BS 410 mesh/inch
0.355			44
0.420	40	35	36
0.500	35	32	30
0.595	30	28	
0.600			25
0.707	25	24	
0.710			22
0.841	20	20	
1.00	18	16	16
1.19	16	14	
1.20			14
1.41	14	12	
1.68	12	10	10
2.00	10	9	8
2.38	8		
2.83	7		
3.36	6		
4.00	5		
4.76	4		4

Table 45

Apertures of Standard Test Sieves

Where μm is the Nominal width aperture of sieve in microns

Sieve type (μm)	Mesh No. *(sieve designation in inches)*
36 DIN	400
37 Tyler, US	400
40 DIN	+ 350
45 BS	350
44 Tyler, US	325
45 DIN	325
53 BS	300
53 Tyler, US	270
62 Tyler, US	250
63 Tyler, US	230
63 BS	240
74 Tyler, US	200
75 BS	200
88 Tyler, US	170
90 BS	170
105 Tyler, US	150/140
105 BS	150
125 BS	120
125 Tyler, US	115
149 Tyler, US	100

Sub-sieve range is 1 μm to 75 μm

Table 45 (continued)

Apertures of Standard Test Sieves

Sieve type (mm)	Mesh No. *(sieve designation in inches)*
150 BS	100
177 Tyler, US	80
180 BS	85
210 BS	72
210 Tyler, US	65/70
250 BS, Tyler, US, DIN	60
300 BS	52
297 Tyler, US	48/50
315 DIN	
355 BS	44
420 BS	36
500 BS	30
600 BS	25
710 BS	22
850 BS	18
1.00 BS,Tyler,US, DIN	16
1.19 Tyler, US	14
1.20 BS	14
1.25 DIN	14
1.40 BS, DIN	12
1.41 Tyler, US	12

Table 45 (continued)

Apertures of Standard Test Sieves

Sieve type (mm)	Mesh No. *(sieve designation in inches)*
1.60 DIN	10
1.68 BS, Tyler, US	10
2.00 Tyler, US, DIN	9
2.00 BS	8
2.3 Tyler, US 8	8
2.40 BS	7
2.50 DIN	8
2.80 BS	6
2.80 DIN	7
2.83 Tyler, US	7
3.15 DIN	6
3.35 BS	5
3.36 Tyler, US	6
4.00 BS	4
4.00 Tyler, US	5
4.76 BS Tyler, US	4
5.60 DIN	3½
5.66 Tyler, US	3½

Table 46

Explosive Limits in air, auto-ignition and Flash Points

Gas or Vapour	LEL % v/v	UEL % v/v	Auto-ignite °C	Flash Point °C
Acetaldehyde	4	60	175	-27
Acetic anhydride	3	10	310	49
Acetone	3	13	460	-18
Acetylene	3	85	330	-18
Acetic acid glacial	4	20	470	40
Ammonia(gas)	16	27	630	11
Aniline	1	11	600	73
Benzene	1	7	560	-11
n-Butane	2	8	400	-60
n-Butyl alcohol	1	11	340	35
Carbon bisulfide	1	44	90	-30
Carbon monoxide	13	74	600	-191
Chlorobenzene	2	10	630	27
Chloroform	-	-	none	none
Cyclohexane	1	8	240	-17
1,4 Dioxan	2	22	180	16
Ethane	3	13	480	-135
Ethyl acetate	2	11	430	-4

Table 46 (continued)

Explosive Limits and Flash Points of chemicals

Gas or Vapour	LEL % v/v in air	UEL % v/v in air	Auto-ignite ^{0}C	Flash Point ^{0}C
Ether	2	48	150	-25
Ethyl alcohol	4	19	360	12
Ethylene (ethene)	3	42	490	-136
n-Heptane	1	7	200	-4
n-Hexane	1	7	200	-22
Hydrogen	4	74	400	-253
Hydrogen sulfide	4	46	270	-83
Methane	5	14	580	-188
Methyl acetate	3	16	450	-13
Methyl alcohol	7	36	380	11
Methylene chloride	12	20	650	none
Methyl ethyl ketone (MEK)	2	10	400	-9
n-Pentane	2	8	300	-40
Petroleum ether 40/60'C	2	11	280	-46
Propane	2	10	460	-104
Propyl alcohols	2	14	400	12/15
Pyridine	2	12	480	20
Sulphur pwd	dust expl	dust expl	240	180
Toluene	1	7	480	4
o-Xylene	1	7	460	22

Table 47

Commodity Properties

Commodity	Density or SG, kg/m³	Auto-ignition °C	Flash Point, °C
Asbestos	320-400	-	-
Charcoal	400	350	
Cement	1290-1600	-	-
Coal, bituminous	760-840	400	130
Coal, anthracite	840-970	450	-
Coke (petcoke)	570-650	600-800	100
Cotton		260	210
Diesel fuel, petr.	810-960	210-400	69
Fuel oil	800-900	200	100/300
Gas oil	800-900	300	30/50
Kerosene	800-900	230	35/80
Lube oil	800-900	400	180/280
Natural gas	700-800	480	
Petrol /gasoline	700-800	280	-43
Paper	80-120grammage	300	
Peat, hay		150-220	
Quartz, sand	1450-2070	-	-
Rubber	1500	260-300	
Salt	1130-1290	-	-
Steel	7850-7900	-	-
Sulphur	800-1130	230	200
Wood, shavings	210-520	150	
Wood, solid	400-1200	350	
Wool		220	

Table 48

Density, Melting & Boiling Point of Metals & Alloys

Element/Metal / alloy	Density (SG)	Melting Point °C	Boiling Point °C
Aluminium (Al)	2.7	650	2500
Antimony (Sb)	6.7	630	1800
Bismuth (Bi)	9.8	270	1600
Brass	8.4	950	-
Bronze	8.0	1000	-
Cast iron	7.5	1200-1350	-
Cadmium (Cd)	8.6	320	800
Copper (Cu)	8.9	1080	2600
Cobalt (Co)	8.7	1480	2900
Chromium (Cr)	7.2	1880	2900
Gold (Au)	19.3	1060	2800
Iron (Fe)	7.8	1530	2900
Lead (Pb)	11.3	330	1700
Manganese (Mn)	7.4	1250	2000
Mercury (Hg)	13.5	-39	360
Molybdenum (Mo)	10.2	2500	4600
Nickel (Ni)	8.8	1450	2700
Platinum (Pt)	21.4	1770	4000
Steel	7.8	1100-1600	-
Silver (Ag)	10.5	960	2200
Sulphur (S)	2.1	110	450
Tin (Sn)	7.3	230	2600
Tungsten (W)	18.8	3400	5600
Zinc (Zn)	7.2	420	900

Table 49

Hardness Scale Mohs

Degree	Mineral	Formula (approx.)
1	Talcum	$Mg_3\{(OH)_2/Si_4O_{10}\}$
2	Gypsum	$CaSO_4.2H_2O$
3	Calcite	$CaCO_3$
4	Fluorspar	CaF_2
5	Apatite	$Ca_5\{(F,Cl,OH)/(PO_4)_3\}$
6	Feldspar	$KAlSi_3O_8$
7	Quartz	SiO_2
8	Topaz	$Al_2\{F_2/SiO_4\}$
9	Corundum	Al_2O_3
10	diamond	C

Table 50

Water Hardness
(degrees of Hardness)

soft water = <1 grain/gal (gpg) = <17ppm
slightly hard =1 to 3.5 grains/gal = 17 to 60 ppm
moderate = 3.5 to 7 grains/gal = 60 to 120 ppm
hard =7 to 10 grains/gal = 120 to 180 ppm
very hard =>10 grains/gal = >180 ppm
Fairfax scale =2 to 10 gpg as slightly to hard
1 mmol/L = 100ppm = 100mg/L $CaCO^3$
1 grain (gpg) = 1 grain $CaCO^3$/US gal = 17.1ppm
1 ppm = 1 mg/L $CaCO_3$
1 ppm = 0.058 grains/US gallon
1 ppm = 0.07 Clark degrees 1 ppm = 0.10 French degrees 1 ppm = 0.056 German degrees
1 grain/US gallon = 1.20 Clark degrees 1 grain/US gallon = 0.958 German degrees

Table 51

Water Hardness conversion factors

1 degree German Hardness (dGH) = 1 part CaO (i.e calcium oxide) in 100, 000 parts water = 10mg/L CaO = 18ppm
1 degree English Hardness (°e) = 1 grain $CaCO_3$ per gallon water = 14ppm
1 degree Clark Hardness (°Clark) = 1 grain as $CaCO_3$ (ie calcium carbonate) per Imperial gallon water = 14ppm
1 degree French Hardness (°fH) = 1 part $CaCO_3$ in 100,000 parts water = 10mg/L $CaCO_3$ = 10ppm = 1 hydrotimetric degree
1.71 degrees French Hardness =1 grain per US gallon water
1^0 GH = 0.056 mg/l $CaCO_3$ = 1ppm
1^0 EH = 0.070 mg/l $CaCO_3$
1^0 FH = 0.100 mg/l $CaCO_3$
1^0 GH = 1.25^0English (EH)
1^0 GH = 1.78^0French (FH)
1^0 EH = 0.80^0German (GH)
1^0 EH = 1.43^0French (FH)
1^0 FH = 0.56^0German (GH)
1^0 FH = 0.70^0English (EH)

Table 52

Gold scale

Carats (Karats)	% gold content by weight (approx.)
24	99.0
22	91.6
18	75.0
9	37.5
8	33.3

Density of pure gold is 19.3 g/cm^3
9 carat gold has approximate density of 12.7 g/cm^3

995 Fine = 995 parts per thousand gold
24 Karats = 1000 Fine
1 Troy ounce gold = 31grams gold
24 grains = 1 Pennyweight (DWT)

Table 53

Wine Industry units
(approximate)

1 keg = 4 to 5 gallons
1 anker = 7 to 8 gallons
1 half aum = 16 to 17 gallons
1 quarter cask = 40 to 41 gallons
1 hogshead = 64 to 65 gallons
1 pipe = 91 to 92 gallons
1 Leaguer = 127 gallons
1 quart or bottle = 26.66 fluid ounces = 0.166 gallon
1 Imperial quart = 40 fluid ounces

Table 54

Alcohol units

(ethyl alcohol-water mixtures)

Alcohol content by % v/v @ 20°C	Alcohol content % mass	% Proof Spirit (UK)	SG (Relative Density) 20°C/20°C
100	100	175.4	0.7904
95	93	166.6	0.8127
90	86	157.8	0.8306
83	77	145	0.8523
75	68	131	0.8740
70	62	122.6	0.8870
60	52	105.1	0.9107
57.1	**49**	**100.0**	**0.9170**
50	**42**	**87.5**	**0.9318**
42	35	73.6	0.9466
34	28	59.6	0.9588
30	25	52.4	0.9640
21	17	36.8	0.9743
16	13	28	0.9795
10	8	17.4	0.9865
5	4	8.7	0.9928
0	0	0	1.000

100 US Proof = 87.5 UK Proof = 50% alcohol by vol

Table 55

Electrochemical Series
(aka Electromotive Series)

Metal	Standard Electrode Potential E° (volts)
Potassium (Anode; -; most active)	-2.92
Calcium	-2.87
Sodium	-2.71
Magnesium	-2.37
Aluminium	-1.66
Manganese	-1.19
Chromium	-0.90
Zinc	-0.76
Iron	-0.44
Tin	-0.14
Lead	-0.13
Hydrogen (REFERENCE)	**0.00**
Tin	+0.15
Bismuth	+0.2
Copper	+0.34
Iron	+0.77
Silver	+0.80
Platinum	+1.2
Gold (Cathode; +; least active)	+1.5

$$Mg_s + Cu_{aq} = Mg_{aq} + Cu_s$$

Table 56

Flame Colours

Carmine Red:	
Lithium compounds.	
Crimson Red:	
Strontium compounds.	
Yellow-Red (brick red):	
Calcium compounds.	
Yellow:	
Sodium compounds, some gold and iron compounds.	
White:	
Magnesium	
White-Green:	
Zinc	
Green:	
Copper compounds (other than halides), thallium, borates, antimony and ammonium compounds.	
Blue-Green:	
Phosphates.	
Yellow-Green:	
Barium, manganese (II), molybdenum.	
Blue (livid blue):	
Lead, selenium, bismuth, cesium, copper, antimony, arsenic.	
Greenish Blue:	
Copper bromide, antimony.	
Violet-purple:	
Potassium compounds.	

Table 57

Flame Emission Spectra

Element	Wavelength Lines in nm
Ag	328, 338
Ba	554, 744, 873
B	345, 452, 548
Ca	423, 554, 622
Co	347, 353, 387
Cr	361, 425, 428
Cs	456, 852, 894
Cu	325, 327, 520
Fe	374, 386,
K	345, 405, 767
Li	323, 460, 671
Mg	285, 371, 383
Mn	280, 403, 543
Na	330, 589, 818
Ni	342, 353, 386
Pb	261, 368, 406
Rb	420, 780, 795
Sr	408, 461, 821
Ti	277, 378, 535

Table 58

Atomic Absorption (flame) Spectra

(Less sensitive alternate wavelengths in brackets)

Element	Absorption wavelength Line in nm	Sensitivity (concentration in µg/ml to yield 1% absorption)
Al	309.3 *(396.1)*	0.8???
Ag	328.1	0.03
As	193.7	0.8
Au	242.8	0.1
B	249.8	8
Ba	553.6 *(350.1)*	0.2
Be	234.9	0.02
Bi	223.1	0.2
Ca	422.7 *(239.9)*	0.02
Cd	228.8 *(326.1)*	0.01
Co	240.7	0.07
Cr	357.9 *(425.4)*	0.06
Cs	852.1	0.1
Cu	324.8 *(327.4)*	0.04
Fe	248.3	0.06
Ge	265.2	2
Hg	253.7	2
In	303.9	0.4
K	766.5	0.01

Table 58 (continued)

Atomic Absorption (flame) Spectra

Element	Absorption wavelength Line in nm	Sensitivity (concentration in µg/ml to yield 1% absorption)
Li	670.8	0.02
Mg	285.2 *(202.5)*	0.003
Mn	279.5 *(403.1)*	0.02
Mo	313.3	0.3
Na	589.0	0.003
Ni	232.0 *(341.5)*	0.07
Pb	217.0 *(283.3)*	0.1
Pt	266.0	1
Sb	217.6	0.3
Se	196.0	0.5
Si	251.6	2
Sn	224.6	0.5
Sr	460.7	0.04
Te	214.3	0.3
Ti	364.3	2
V	318.5	0.9
W	255.1	6
Zn	213.9 *(307.6)*	0.009
Zr	360.1	9

Table 59

Flame and Heat Temperatures

Source	Temperature °C
Fluorescent light	60 - 80
Incandescent light	100 - 300
Tungsten halogen light	600 - 900
Wood / charcoal	1000 - 1500
Hotplate / stove element	400 - 600
Match	600 - 800
Oven, very slow cooking	120 (250°F)
Oven, slow cooking	150 (300°F)
Oven, moderate cooking	180 (350°F)
Oven, hot cooking	220 (425°F)
Oven, very hot cooking	240 (460°F)
Cigarettes	200 - 600
Candle flame	600 - 1200
Lightning	30 000
Bunsen burner (depending on gas mixture type)	400 - 1500
Industrial furnace	1700
Hydrogen/air	+-2000
Carbon monoxide/air	+-2300
Air/Acetylene	+-2600
Electrical spark	+-1200
Electrical arcing	+-3600
Oxygen/Acetylene	+-3300
Nitrous Oxide/Acetylene	+-2900

Table 60

Solvents for UV Spectrophotometry

Chemical/Solvent	Polarity	UV Cutoff (nm) in 1cm cuvette
Acetone		330
Acetonitrile	polar	190/210
n-Pentane	non-polar	190
Hexane (UV grade)	non-polar	195
Cyclohexane	non-polar	200
Methyl alcohol, anhydrous	polar	205
Isopropyl alcohol	polar	205/210
Ethanol	polar	210
Methylene chloride	non-polar	233
Chloroform	semi-polar	245
Ethyl acetate	semi-polar	256/260
Pyridine	polar	330
Toluene		254
Water		190

When doing UV spectrophotometry measurements, ensure that the cuvettes are quartz and not glass or plastic!

Table 61

Solvents for general use

Solute or substrate	Solvent
Polystyrene	Methyl isobutyl ketone (MIBK)
Cellulose acetate	MIBK
Cellulose acetate butyrate	MIBK
Polyacrylonitrile	Dimethylformamide (DMF)
polycarbonate	DMF
Polyvinylchloride (PVC)	DMF
PVC/PVA copolymer	cylohexanone
Polyamide	60% formic acid
Polyethers	methanol
Perspex	dichloromethane
uPVC	Methyl ethyl ketone
Bitumen	benzene
Plastics, most	acetone
Rubbers, most	cyclohexane

Table 62

Ionic Conductance Values

(Equivalent at infinite dilution in water @ 25°C)

S.cm²/mol

Cation	A^+		Anion	A^-
H^+	350		NO_2^-	72
Na^+	50		OH^-	199
K^+	74		F^-	55
Li^+	39		Cl^-	76
NH_4^+	74		Br^-	78
Ag^+	62		I^-	77
Cs^+	77		IO_3^-	41
Sr^{++}	119		IO_4^-	55
Ca^{++}	119		ClO_4^-	67
Ba^{++}	128		ClO_3^-	65
Mg^{++}	106		BrO_3^-	56
Zn^{++}	106		$HCOO^-$	55
Cu^{++}	107		HCO_3^-	45
Pb^{++}	142		CO_3^{--}	139
Ni^{++}	106		SO_4^{--}	160
Ba^{++}	127		PO_4^{---}	207
Fe^{++}	108			
Fe^{+++}	204			
La^{+++}	210			
Al^{+++}	183			

Table 63

Conductivity cell constants, range

Cell constant to use (K)	Range of liquid/sample	Example
0.01	<20 μS/cm	clean water
0.1	0.5 μS/cm to 200 μS/cm	clear effluent
1.0	5 μS/cm to 10 mS/cm	Trade effluent
10	1 mS/cm to 100 mS/cm	high electrolytes

Table 64

Solubility of Compounds in Water

Compounds (inorganic)	Solubility (at room temperature)
Sodium, Potassium, Ammonium compounds	All soluble
Nitrates	All soluble
Chlorides	All soluble, except silver chloride, lead chloride, mercurous chloride, cuprous chloride
Sulphates	All soluble, except barium sulphate, lead sulphate, calcium sulphate, strontium sulphate
Sulphides	All insoluble, except sodium sulphide, potassium sulphide, ammonium sulphide, barium sulphide, calcium sulphide
Carbonates	All insoluble, except sodium carbonate, potassium carbonate, ammonium carbonate
Bicarbonates	All soluble
Oxides and hydroxides	Sodium, potassium, calcium, barium are slightly soluble

Table 65

Dilution Formula

(also known as Pearson's Square or Rectangle)

A \		↗ D
	C	
B /		↘ E

Let A and B be the strength of the constituents in descending order of strength respectively.

Let C be the strength required of the diluted substance or liquid.

Then E = A-C = parts or mass of B to be taken

and D = C -B = parts or mass of A to be taken.

For dilution by volume:

D = mass of A divided by density of A = volume A to be taken.

E = mass of B divided by density of B = volume B to be taken.

Table 65 (continued)

Dilution Formula

EXAMPLE:
Prepare a 20% solution of hydrochloric acid from a 31% (concentrated) bottle of hydrochloric acid of density 1.155.

Now A = 31%
B = 0% because its water.
C = 20% (the required strength of solution wanted).
Density HCl is 1.555
Density water is 1.00

Parts by mass: Parts by volume:

31		↗ 20		20/1.155	=	17.32 A
	20					
0 ⁄		↘ 11		11/1.00	=	11.00 water

i.e. add 17.32ml acid to 11.0ml water to get a 20% diluted acid solution of about 28ml total volume.

Table 66

Drying Agents - Desiccants
In increasing order of moisture absorption

Desiccant solid	Formula	Water content of air in equilibrium, in mg/l at 25^{0}C
Copper sulphate	$CuSO_4$	1.4 *poor desiccant*
Zinc chloride, fused	$ZnCl_2$	0.8
Calcium chloride	$CaCl_2$	0.2
Sodium hydroxide	$NaOH$	0.2
Magnesium oxide	MgO	0.01
Calcium sulphate	$CaSO_4$	0.01
Sulphuric acid, conc.	H_2SO_4	0.003
Aluminium oxide	Al_2O_3	0.003
Potassium hydroxide	KOH	0.002
Silica Gel (Blue-dried)	$(SiO_2)_x$	0.002
Molecular sieves	-	0.001
Phosphorus pentoxide, flakes	P_2O_5	0.00003 *best desiccant*

Table 67

Constant Humidity Solutions

Solute Saturated Solution	Formula	(Approx.) Relative Humidity above solution at 20°C
Lead nitrate	$Pb(NO_3)_2$	98
Sodium carbonate	$Na_2CO_3.10H_2O$	92
Potassium chloride	KCl	86
Ammonium sulphate	$(NH_4)_2SO_4$	80
Sodium chloride	$NaCl$	76
Sodium nitrite	$NaNO_2$	65
Ammonium nitrate	NH_4NO_3	63
Calcium nitrate	$Ca(NO_3)_2.4\,H_2O$	55
Potassium thiocyanate	$KSCN$	47
Zinc nitrate	$Zn(NO_3)_2.6\,H_2O$	42
Calcium chloride	$CaCl_2.6H_2O$	35
Potassium acetate	CH_3COOK	20
Lithium chloride	$LiCl.\,H_2O$	15

Table 68

Freezing Mixtures

Components	(Approx.) Temperature, $^\circ$C
100g water + 100g ice	0
100g water + 30g ammonium chloride	-3
100g water + 75g sodium nitrate	-5
100g ice + 28g barium chloride	-7
100g water + 35g sodium chloride	-10
100g ice + 30g sodium chloride	-20
100g ice + magnesium chloride	-33
100g ice + 122g calcium chloride hexahydrate	-40
100g ice + 144g calcium chloride hexahydrate	-55
Alcohol + dry ice (solid CO_2)	-70
Chloroform+ dry ice (solid CO_2)	-77
Acetone + dry ice (solid CO_2)	-85
Ether + dry ice (solid CO_2)	-100

Table 69

Nomenclature of Acids

Structure acid	Wording	Example
Most common	------ic	HCL Hydrochlor**ic** acid
Contains more oxygen	per--------ic	$HClO_4$ Perchlor**ic** acid
Contains less oxygen	--------ous	$HCLO_2$ Chlor**ous** acid
Contains even less oxygen	hypo----ous	HCLO **Hypo**chlor**ous** acid

Table 70

Chemical Reactions

Acid + base = salt + water
Acid + alcohol = ester + water
Halogen + metal = salt
Acid anhydrides + water = acid
Acid oxides + water = acid
Metal + acid = salt + hydrogen
Combination or synthesis: A + B = AB
Decomposition: AB = A + B
Substitution or single displacement: A + BC = AC + B
Double displacement or double decomposition: AB + CD = AD + CB
Redox: $A + B = A_{\text{reduced form}} + B_{\text{oxidised form}}$
Combustion: $A_{\text{combustible form}} + O_2 = CO_2 + H_2O$
Hydrolysis: $A^- + H_2O = HA_{\text{aqueous}} + OH^-_{\text{base}}$

Table 71

Analytical & Stoichiometric Factors

To report as	Test result obtained	X Factor
Al	Al_2O_3	0.5293
Al_2O_3	Al	1.8895
Ca	$CaCO_3$	0.4004
Ca	CaO	0.7147
CaO	Ca	1.399
$CaSO_4$	$BaSO_4$	0.5833
Cr_2O_3	Cr	1.462
CuO	Cu	1.252
Fe_2O_3	Fe	1.430
H_2SO_4	$BaSO_4$	0.4202
K_2O	K	1.2051
MgO	Mg	1.658
NH_3	NH_4	0.9441

Table 71 (continued)

Analytical & Stoichiometric Factors

To report as	Test result obtained	X Factor
Na	Cl	0.6485
NaCl	AgCl	0.4078
NaCl	Cl	1.6488
NaCl	Na	2.5413
P_2O_5	P	2.2914
P	P_2O_5	0.4364
P	PO_4	0.3261
PO_4	P_2O_5	1.338
PO_4	P	3.0665
PbO_2	Pb	0.8662
SO_2	$BaSO_4$	0.2745
SO_3	$BaSO_4$	0.3430
SO_4	$BaSO_4$	0.4116
ZnO	Zn	1.245

Table 72

Oxygen Levels

Environment	% Oxygen level in air
Dry air	20.9
Exhaust breathe of human	18
Safe to breathe	18.5 to 23.5
Unsafe for humans, anoxia begins	below 16
Fire hazard, enhanced combustion	above 24
Fire / oxidation to occur (minimum to support combustion)	above 10
Prevention of Fire or explosion	below 5
Inert atmosphere in enclosed container	below 5

Table 73

Electromagnetic Spectrum

Type radiation	Wavelength, in meters
Gamma rays	10^{-12} to 10^{-14}
X-rays	10^{-11} to 10^{-10}
Ultraviolet rays	10^{-8} *(190 to 380 nm)*
Visible light: *Violet* *Indigo* *Blue* *Green* *Yellow* *Orange* *Red*	10^{-6} *(400 to 420 nm)* *(420 to 440 nm)* *(440 to 490 nm)* *(490 to 570 nm)* *(570 to 585nm)* *(585 to 620 nm)* *(620to 780 nm)*
Infrared rays	10^{-6} to 10^{-4}
microwave	10^{-2}
radar	10^{-2}
FM radio	10^{1}
TV signals	10^{1}
Shortwave radio	10^{2}
AM radio	10^{4}

Table 74

Valency of an Element

Element	Atomic Number	Symbol	Valency
Aluminium	13	Al	3
Arsenic	33	As	3,5
Barium	56	Ba	2
Beryllium	4	Be	2
Bismuth	83	Bi	3,5
Boron	5	B	3
Bromine	35	Br	1
Calcium	20	Ca	2
Carbon	6	C	2,4
Chlorine	17	Cl	1
Chromium	24	Cr	3,6
Cobalt	27	Co	2
Copper	29	Cu	1,2
Fluorine	9	F	1
Gold	79	Au	3
Hydrogen	1	H	1
Iodine	53	I	1
Iron	26	Fe	2,3
Lead	82	Pb	2,4
Lithium	3	Li	1
Magnesium	12	Mg	2
Manganese	25	Mn	2,3,4,6

Table 74 (continued)

Valency of an element

Element	Atomic Number.	Symbol	Valency
Mercury	80	Hg	1,2
Molybdenum	42	Mo	6
Nickel	28	Ni	2
Nitrogen	7	N	1,2,3
Oxygen	8	O	2
Phosphorus	15	P	3,5
Platinum	78	Pt	2,4
Potassium	19	K	1
Silicon	14	Si	4
Silver	47	Ag	1
Sodium	11	Na	1
Strontium	38	Sr	2
Sulphur	16	S	2,4,6
Tin	50	Sn	2,4
Titanium	22	Ti	4
Uranium	92	U	6
Zinc	30	Zn	2

Table 75

Valency of an ion

Free radical or ion	Symbol	Valency
Acetate	$C_2H_3O_2$	-1
Bicarbonate	HCO_3	-1
Bisulphate	HSO_4	-1
Carbonate	CO_3	-2
Chlorate	CLO_3	-1
Chloride	CL	-1
Chlorite	CLO_2	-1
Chromate	CrO_4	-2
Cyanide	CN	-1
Hydride	H	-1
Hydroxide	OH	-1
Hypochlorite	CLO	-1
Nitrate	NO_3	-1
Nitride	N	-3
Nitrite	NO_2	-1
Perchlorate	CLO_4	-1
Permanganate	MnO_4	-1
Phosphate	PO_4	-3
Phosphide	P	-3
Sulphide	S	-2
Sulphite	SO_3	-2
Sulphate	SO_4	-2
Thiocyanates	SCN	-1
Thiosulphate	S_2O_3	-2

Table 76

Atomic Mass

Element	Atomic Mass		Element	Atomic Mass
Aluminium Al	26.982		Carbon C	12.011
Antimony Sb	121.760		Cerium Ce	140.120
Arsenic As	74.922		Chlorine Cl	35.453
Barium Ba	137.330		Chromium Cr	51.996
Berylium Be	9.0122		Cobalt Co	58.933
Bismuth Bi	208.981		Copper Cu	63.546
Boron B	10.810		Fluorine F	18.998
Bromine Br	79.904		Gallium Ga	69.723
Cadmium Cd	112.411		Gold Au	196.97
Caesium Cs	132.905		Iodine I	126.90
Calcium Ca	40.078		Iron Fe	55.845

Table 76 (continued)

Atomic Mass

Element	Atomic Mass	Element	Atomic Mass
Lead Pb	207.20	Potassium K	39.098
Lithium Li	6.940	Selenium Se	78.960
Magnesium Mg	24.305	Silicon Si	28.085
Manganese Mn	54.938	Silver Ag	107.870
Mercury Hg	200.59	Sodium Na	22.989
Molybdenum Mo	95.960	Strontium Sr	87.620
Nickel Ni	58.693	Sulphur S	32.060
Nitrogen N	14.007	Thallium Tl	204.380
Oxygen O	16.000	Tin Sb	118.710
Phosphorus P	30.974	Titanium Ti	47.867
Platinum Pt	195.08	Zinc Zn	65.380

Glossary and Scientific Terms

- ACIDS & BASES, two classes of chemical compounds that display generally opposite characteristics. Acids taste sour, turn litmus (a pink dye derived from lichens) red, and will react with metals to produce hydrogen gas. Bases taste bitter, turn litmus blue, and feel slippery to the touch. When aqueous (water) solutions of an acid and a base are combined, a neutralisation reaction occurs. This reaction is characteristically very rapid and generally produces water and a salt. For example, sulphuric acid (H_2SO_4), and sodium hydroxide (NaOH), yield water (H_2O) and the salt sodium sulphate (Na_2SO_4):

$$H_2SO_4 + 2NaOH = 2H_2O + Na_2SO_4$$

(A stoichiometric equation)

1 molecule H_2SO_4 + 2 molecules NaOH = 2 molecules H_2O + 1 molecule Na_2SO_4

- ALLOTROPES of an element are the different physical forms (crystalline or molecular) of that element; e.g. carbon has two allotropes, namely diamond and graphite.

- ACCURACY is where the test results are as close to the "true" value or reference value of a test procedure as possible; as compared to the precision of the test results.

- ABSOLUTE VISCOSITY (in centipoises) is equal to kinematic viscosity (in centistokes) multiplied by density.

- AMPHOTERIC is a substance or compound that can chemically act as an acid or as a base.

- AMORPHOUSc is a substance that has no definite shape or form, it is non-crystalline.

- APOTHECARY units are used in the pharmacy field and are closely related with the English troy system of weights.

- AQUA REGIA is a mixture of nitric and hydrochloric acids (1:4). It dissolves the noble metals (gold and platinum), hence its name (aqua means water and regia means royalty).

- ATOM is the smallest part of a specific element. Atoms of the same element (e.g. sodium) are identical in physical and chemical properties and have same atomic number (the number of electrons or protons). An atom consists essentially of a nucleus (containing protons and neutrons) surrounded by electrons.

- ATOMIC MASS of an atom is the number of protons plus number of neutrons. The atomic mass used in calculations and given in the Periodic Table is a weighted average (as found in nature) of the atomic masses of the isotopes of the elements.

- AVOIRDUPOIS weight unit is a system of weights based on the pound (lb), which contains 16 ounces or 7000 grains. 100 pounds (US) or 112 pounds (British) is equal to 1 hundredweight and 20 hundredweights equals 1 ton.

- BILLION is a million million in the SI system of units, i.e. it is 1 000 000 000 000. But in the USA a billion is 1 000 million, i.e. 1 000 000 000.

- CAUSTIC is a substance that is said to cause corrosion of metals or destruction of organic matter; chemically sodium hydroxide (caustic soda) is considered to be caustic; also anything that has alkaline properties may be considered to be caustic.

- CHEMICAL; the word CHEMICAL is, unfortunately, used in everyday language to describe a hazardous substance. This is scientifically incorrect as all matter is composed of chemicals, there are good chemicals such as fresh food, vitamins, medicine, water, etc., and there are bad chemicals such as cyanides, DDT, etc.

- CHROMATOGRAPHY is a technique used for separating and identifying various anions, cations and organic compounds; e.g. TLC, HPLC, GC-MS.

- COEFFICIENT OF VARIANCE (of a mean) is a statistical representation of the precision of a test result. The function is: (standard deviation / mean) x 100%.

- COMPOUND is made of elements in fixed proportions, e.g. NaCl, Na_2CO_3. There are billions of natural compounds and new synthetic compounds are being made every day.

- DE-IONISED WATER is relatively pure water made by passing water through ion-exchange resins to remove (adsorb) soluble inorganic salts; however it does not remove organic impurities and dissolved gases in the water. This type of water should not be used for microbiological tests. For ultra-pure water, the water can be first passed through a de-ioniser then distilled followed by a reverse osmosis unit.
  Pure water is NOT suitable for drinking!

- DELIQUESCENCE is where solid substances absorb water from the air and dissolve in it to form a liquid.

- DENSITY is by definition, mass per unit volume. There are basically three types of density: Density in vacuo, True Density, and Apparent Density. The former two are tested by hydrometer and the latter one is tested by a pyconometer or SG Bottle. The units for density are in mass/volume and at a specific temperature, e.g. kg/litre at 20°C.

- DEVARDA'S ALLOY is used as catalyst in test for (Total) Nitrogen (by Kjeldahl method) to reduce nitrates and nitrites to ammonia.

- DETECTION LIMIT is that lowest concentration of a solute or substance mass that is obtained to distinguish it from background noise or blank solutions. It is usually taken to be three times the measuring instrumental background noise or signal.

- DILATANT liquids is where its viscosity increases as the shear rate increases, e.g. clay slurries.

- DISTILLED WATER is relatively pure water made by boiling the water and condensing the steam; this should preferably be done in an all-glass water still, otherwise a stainless steel water still. This water contains no dissolved gases but does readily absorb carbon dioxide from the atmosphere, thus changing its pH (ultra-pure water should have a pH of 7.0). However, this water could be high in silicates due to the glass apparatus. Sometimes the water is triple distilled to obtain a conductivity of less than 0.5 microSiemen per centimetre. Pure water is NOT suitable for drinking!

- EFFLORESCENCE is where hydrates are so unstable that their "water of crystallisation" is given up to the atmosphere, to form a type of surface crystallisation or deposit.

- ELECTROMOTIVE SERIES or ELECTROCHEMICAL SERIES is a series (list) of elements arranged in order of their electrode potentials (or ability to replace metals from one another when in their salt form). The series is K, Ca, Na, Mg, Al, Zn, Cd, Fe, Ni, Sn, Pb, H_2, Cu, Hg, Ag, Pt and Au (where H_2 is taken to be zero). Thus, a copper salt will replace a zinc metal.

- ELECTROLYSIS is a process in which an electrolyte (salts in solution) is decomposed by means of an electric current. The more dilute a solution the greater the degree of ionisation. Hydrogen or the metal always appears at the cathode (negative electrode); the oxygen or non-metal always appears at the anode (positive electrode). Example, water is split into hydrogen gas and oxygen gas.

- ELEMENT is made of atoms; there are 117 (or more) elements known and these are listed in a chart (known as the Periodic Table), in order of their specific chemical and physical properties. Example: H, He, Li, Be, B, etc.

- EQUIVALENT WEIGHT of an element is the weight of the element which will combine with 8 parts by weight of oxygen, or the equivalent of 8 parts by weight of oxygen. Note that equivalent weight of element x valency of element = atomic weight of element.

- ESCHKA'S COMPOUND or flux for (total) sulphur determinations; 2 parts calcined light magnesia thoroughly mixed with 1 part anhydrous sodium carbonate.

- FARADAY is the unit for quantity of electricity which will liberate the gram equivalent weight of an element from solution. 1 faraday = 96500 coulombs.

- FARADAY'S LAWS:

  1st: The masses of substances liberated at the electrodes on electrolysis of an electrolyte, are directly proportional to the current and time for which it flows.

  2nd: When the same current is passed through different electrolytes for the same time, the weights of substances liberated at the electrodes will be proportional to their chemical equivalents.

- FUNCTIONAL GROUPS are the identifiable groups of atoms exhibiting characteristic properties or reactions of a compound. For example alcohols have the –OH group.

- GALVANIC SERIES (or electropotential series) determines the nobility of metals and semi-metals. When two metals are submerged in an electrolyte, while electrically connected, the less noble (base) will experience galvanic corrosion. The rate of corrosion is determined by the electrolyte and the difference in nobility. The difference can be measured as a difference in voltage potential.

- HEAVY METALS are usually classed as those elements that have a density of greater than 4, e.g. Cu, Zn, Cr, Hg, Fe, Pb, Pt, Ag.

- HETEROGENEOUS matter is NOT uniform in composition but consists of two or more physically distinct properties. Each physically distinct homogeneous portion of a heterogeneous mixture is called a phase. Example: yoghurt containing fruit particles, pure orange juice with pulp.

- HOMOGENEOUS matter is uniform throughout its composition with respect to its chemical and physical properties. Example: salt, sugar, flour, cement.

- HOMOLOGOUS SERIES is a series (list) of related compounds that have the same functional group but differ in their formula by a fixed group of atoms. For example, the carboxylic acids: formic acid (HCOOH); acetic acid (CH_3COOH); propionic acid (C_2H_5COOH).

- HYGROSCOPY is where substances absorb water from the atmosphere but not sufficient to dissolve in it.

- IODIMETRY is a direct titration test method in which a standard solution of iodine is used to titrate strong reductants, usually in neutral or slightly acidic solution.

- IODOMETRY is an indirect titration test method in which oxidising agents are determined by reacting with an excess of iodide; where the iodine liberated is titrated with a standard reductant such as a solution of sodium thiosulphate, usually in a slightly acidic media.

- ISOTOPES of an element have same number of protons, but different number of neutrons, hence different atomic masses.

- LACHRYMATORY causes crying, e.g. benzyl chloride.

- MCFARLAND EQUIVALENCE TURBIDITY STANDARDS are used as standards in adjusting densities of bacterial suspensions.

- MENISCUS is the curved surface of a liquid when the liquid is in a narrow tube such as a burette or pipette.

- A MILLIARD number is 1,000,000,000; also referred to in the USA as a billion. In the UK a billion is 1,000,000,000,000.

- MOLECULE is the smallest part of a compound and is formed by the combination of two or more elements. Example: a molecule of water is H_2O.

- NEPHELOMETRY is the measurement of the intensity of the scattered light at right angles to the direction of the incident light, as a function of a turbid liquid.

- NESSLERIMETRY is a form of colorimetry where a comparison of two colours of two solutions (liquids) in Nessler Tubes or Cells, are made; e.g. the Lovibond Comparator ®.

- NEWTONIAN liquids is where its viscosity remains constant regardless of the applied shear rate or agitation, e.g. oils.

- NEUTRON is an electrically neutral part of the nucleus of an atom.

- NORMALITY, MOLARITY, MOLALITY AND FORMALITY are specific concentrations of standardized solutions used in titrimetric/volumetric analysis.

- OMEGA FATTY ACIDS: omega-3 and omega-6 are polyunsaturated; omega-9 are monounsaturated.

- PARTS PER MILLION generally indicates 1 part of a substance (solute) in a million parts of another substance (solution).

- PERCENTAGE in a concentration sense, indicates 1 part of a substance (solute) in a hundred parts of another substance (solution).

- PERIODIC TABLE is a list or chart of all the known elements in numerical order according to their atomic numbers.

- pH is an arbitrary unit of acidity or alkalinity on a scale of 0 to 14; where 7 to 0 is increasing in acidity (decreasing in alkalinity) and 7 to 14 is decreasing in acidity (increasing in alkalinity). By definition pH is the log of the hydrogen ion concentration:

  Neutral pH = 7.0 = $10^{-7.0}$ grams H^+ per litre concentration. Example: pH of 6.6 has a hydrogen ion concentration of $10^{-6.6}$ g/l.

- PHOTOMETRY:

  Absorbance = A = $-\log T$;   where T = %Transmission of light

- POLARISATION is where a source of monochromatic light (the sodium D line at a wavelength of 589.3nm) is passed through a solution of an optically active substance (such as sucrose) which rotates the plane of polarisation; where the degree of rotation is dependent upon the amount of the substance in solution. Temperature is critical and is usually at 20°C.

- PRECISION is where the test results are as close to each other as possible under the conditions of the test; compared to accuracy of a test result.

- PEROXIDE concentration of hydrogen peroxide (H_2O_2) is expressed in VOLUMES OF OXYGEN that it can evolve; e.g. 3% solution is 10 volumes oxygen

- PROTON is an electrically positive part of the nucleus of an atom.

- PSEUDOPLASTIC liquids are those where its viscosity decreases as the shear rate increases, e.g. gels.

- SENSITIVITY of an AAS instrument reading is the solution concentration or mass that produces a signal of 0.0044 Absorbance or 1% Absorption. (cf. DETECTION LIMIT).

- SUBLIMATION is a process where a substance changes form from a solid directly to its gaseous phase without changing to its intermediate liquid form.

- QUALITATIVE ANALYSIS involves determining what elements or compounds are present in a substance.

- QUANTITATIVE ANALYSIS involves determining the quantities (amount) of each element or compound present in a substance.

- REAGENT is something (a chemical liquid or powder) that will react with something else (a chemical liquid, or powder) to produce a product.

- RELATIVE DENSITY is same as Specific Gravity.

- RELATIVE CENTRIFUGAL FORCE for a centrifuge is:

$$rcf = (11.18 \times 10^{-6}) \times R \times N$$

where   R = radius of the rotating arm in cm
N = rotation speed in rpm

- REPEATABILITY is where a repeat test, on the same sample, produces the same result (or within the methodology's degree of precision) as the previous result, in the same laboratory using same analyst and methodology; as compared to reproducibility in another laboratory. An analyst is said to be highly competent if he/she gets the same test results when the same sample is tested separately several times, under the same conditions of test.

- REPRODUCIBILITY is where tests are done on a series of identical samples or test items and produces similar or acceptable results, using different analysts, instruments and different laboratories, BUT using the same test method; as compared to repeatability in same laboratory. A test method is said to have a high degree of reproducibility if the same result is obtained on identical samples but tested by two or more laboratories.

- SATURATED SOLUTION is a solution which has a maximum amount of solute in a given volume of solvent, at a given temperature.

- SOLUTION is a homogeneous mixture of two or more substances, which may be solids (e.g. copper and zinc in brass), liquids (e.g. nitric acid in water), gases (e.g. oxygen and nitrogen in air), or a combination of these (e.g. salt in water).

- SOLVENT is a substance (major phase, e.g. water) which dissolves a solute substance (minor phase, e.g. salt) to make a solution (single phase, e.g. saltwater).

- SOLUTE is the substance (e.g. sugar) that dissolves into a solvent (e.g. water).

- SPECIFIC GRAVITY (SG) is a ratio of density of a substance (at temperature T1) to the density of another substance, usually water (at temperature T2). Thus, the SG of a substance at T1/T2, is numerically same as Density of that substance at T1 if the other substance is water at T2=4°C). SG has no units as it is a ratio, but it is always reported at two temperatures, e.g. 20°C/4°C.

- SPECTROPHOTOMETRY is the measurement of the transmitted light after passing through a media (sample solution) at a specific wavelength.

- STANDARD DEVIATION is the square root of the average of the squares of deviations about the mean of a set of data. Thus, Standard Deviation (s) is a statistical measure of spread or variability of a set of data.

- STOICHIOMETRY is the relative proportions in which elements form compounds, or ratios in which substances react with one another. Example:

$$H_2SO_4 + 2NaOH = 2H_2O + Na_2SO_4$$

- Stowage Factor (SF) is the volume occupied by unit weight of cargo; usually expressed in cubic meter per tonne (metric).

- THIXOTROPIC liquids are those liquids where its viscosity decreases as the shear rate increases, similar to pseudoplastic liquids but its viscosity does not return to its original value, e.g. peanut butter.

- TURBIDIMETRY is the measurement of the intensity of the transmitted light as a function of the concentration of a turbid liquid.

- TRITURATE means to rub, crush, grind, or pound into fine particles or a powder.

- TROY weights are usually used for measurements of precious metals.

- VALENCY is the combining power of an atom or radical, equal to the number of hydrogen atoms that the atom could combine with or displace in a chemical compound (where hydrogen has a valency of 1); e.g. sulphuric acid H_2SO_4 has a valency of 2.

- Viscosity, Dynamic, has units of $N.s/m^2$ or poises; whereas Kinematic has units of m^2/s or stokes.

- Volume Correction Factors (VCF), aka Density Correction Factors, are used to compensate for the expansion or contraction of materials when there is a change in temperature; this has to be taken into consideration when measuring volumes of liquids. (cf. densities and Stowage Factor)

- VOLUMETRIC ANALYSIS: NORMAL SOLUTION (N) contains 1 gram equivalent per litre of solution. CONCENTRATION in grams per litre (g/l) = N x equivalent weight. $V_1N_1 = V_2N_2$

- WAVELENGTH or WAVE NUMBER:

Wavelength in nm = 1/wave number in cm^{-1}

E. & O. E.

INDEX

A

B

C

D

E

F

G

H

I

O

P

Q

R

S

T

NOTES

NOTES